LETTERS TO THE WEARY

MARK & JENNIFER SOWERSBY

All Scripture quotations, unless otherwise indicated, are taken from the Holy Bible, New International Version®, NIV®. Copyright ©1973, 1978, 1984, 2011 by Biblica, Inc.™ Used by permission of Zondervan. All rights reserved worldwide. www.zondervan.com. The "NIV" and "New International Version" are trademarks registered in the United States Patent and Trademark Office by Biblica, Inc.™

Scripture quotations marked ESV are from the ESV® Bible (The Holy Bible, English Standard Version®), copyright © 2001 by Crossway, a publishing ministry of Good News Publishers. Used by permission. All rights reserved.

Scripture quotations marked NLT are taken from the Holy Bible, New Living Translation, copyright ©1996, 2004, 2015 by Tyndale House Foundation. Used by permission of Tyndale House Publishers, a Division of Tyndale House Ministries, Carol Stream, Illinois 60188. All rights reserved.

Scripture quotations marked NKJV are taken from the New King James Version®. Copyright © 1982 by Thomas Nelson. Used by permission. All rights reserved.

Scripture quotations marked KJV are taken from the King James Version of the Bible. Public domain.

Scripture quotations marked TLB are taken from The Living Bible copyright © 1971. Used by permission of Tyndale House Publishers, Carol Stream, Illinois 60188. All rights reserved.

Scripture quotations marked NASB are taken from the (NASB®) New American Standard Bible®, Copyright © 1960, 1971, 1977, 1995, 2020 by The Lockman Foundation. Used by permission. All rights reserved. www.lockman.org.

This publication is meant as a source of valuable information for the reader, however it is not meant as a substitute for direct expert assistance. If such level of assistance is required, the services of a competent professional should be sought.

Copyright © 2025 Mark Sowersby

All rights reserved. No part of this publication may be reproduced, distributed, or transmitted in any form or by any means, including photocopying, recording, or other electronic or mechanical methods, without the prior written permission of the publisher, except in the case of brief quotations embodied in critical reviews and certain other noncommercial uses permitted by copyright law. For permission requests, write to the publisher, addressed "Attention: Permissions Coordinator," at the email address below.

Paperback: 978-1-951475-39-0
Ebook: 978-1-951475-40-6

First paperback edition: January 2025

Cover Art and Layout by Amanda Blake Design

Arrow Press Publishing
www.arrowpresspublishing.com
info@arrowpresspublishing.com

CONTENTS

Day 1 | They Stole My "No"	8
Day 2 | The Rope Bridge	14
Day 3 | Forgive Yourself or Love Yourself	19
Day 4 | Jesus Paid it All	24
Day 5 | The Last Straw	29
Day 6 | Perspective	35
Day 7 | Come to Me	41
Day 8 | Chameleon	46
Day 9 | What the Enemy Meant for Evil	51
Day 10 | Love Lifts Us Up	56
Day 11 | You Are Loved	61
Day 12 | Garment of Praise	66
Day 13 | The Big But	72
Day 14 | Safe Place	77
Day 15 | Return to Sender, Address Unknown	82

Day 16 | Know That I Am God	88
Day 17 | The Good Seed	93
Day 18 | Not Just a Fan	98
Day 19 | Gold and Silver	104
Day 20 | Deconstruction	109
Day 21 | Sleepless	116

INTRODUCTION

When asked, "What is more important: Prayer or Reading the Bible?" I ask, "What is more important: Breathing in or Breathing out?" – Charles Spurgeon

Prayer and reading God's Word are great gifts given to the body of Christ. As I grew in my faith, I realized how important and how valuable these two practices were and still are. The Bible is not just a monologue; it's a dialogue where we see and learn to trust the nature and character of the Lord. The Bible is truly a light unto our path.

> *Your word is a lamp for my feet, a light on my path.*
>
> **PSALM 119:105**

We need to pray consistently, which enables us to move confidently. Paul, who wrote much of the New Testament, encourages us,

> *Continue steadfastly in prayer, being watchful in it with thanksgiving. At the same time, pray also for us, that God may open to us a door for the word, to declare the mystery*

> of Christ, on account of which I am in prison—that I may make it clear, which is how I ought to speak. Walk in wisdom toward outsiders, making the best use of the time. Let your speech always be gracious, seasoned with salt, so that you may know how you ought to answer each person.
>
> **COLOSSIANS 4:2–6 ESV**

What a beautiful explanation Paul gives about prayer. Each one of the principles of prayer is expressed in our prayers today. This Scripture challenges us to

1. Continue to pray (Colossians 4:2a).
2. Be watchful and thankful (Colossians 4:2b).
3. Pray for friends and loved ones (Colossians 4:3a).
4. Look for opportunities to share God's Word (Colossians 4:3b).
5. Preach the gospel clearly (Colossians 4:4).
6. Walk in wisdom (Colossians 4:5a).
7. Organize time carefully (Colossians 4:5b).
8. Speak graciously (Colossians 4:6a).
9. Be ready to give an answer about your faith (Colossians 4:6b).

While we use different words than Paul did and emphasize different expressions, at the core, we also pray for our family, and for wisdom, direction, guidance, opportunity, and humility. There are times we find ourselves in a season of prayer and fasting - a time of giving up something as we focus more on our relationship with God. Fasting is an act of surrender and discipline, not something we do to try to twist God's arm or to get what we want.

In this *Letters to the Weary* devotional you will find twenty-one letters to encourage you through the testimony of someone who has walked through adversity and found strength in the Word of God—who has learned to pray not because it was easy, but because it was right. Over the next twenty-one days, as you take time to go on a journey in your prayer life and your Bible reading, our hope is that your journey will encourage you, challenge you, and bring you to a deeper place of prayer and Bible reading. Each devotion is a combination of reflection and testimony that will have Scripture wrapped within it, as well as what we are calling The Big Question. It is a thought-provoking question for you or your group to answer, and a section for you to record any thoughts, prayers, or reflections.

Let's pray together as we begin.

Lord, we thank You for Your grace and mercy. I pray today for those who are ready for Your Word and pray that we will trust in Your ways and humbly give ourselves to Your will. Teach us to seek You first, for we know Your ways are higher than our ways. Bless the reader and bring them to a place of peace, hope, and forgiveness that is only found in You and through You. Amen.

Love,
Mark & Jennifer

THEY STOLE MY "NO"

Dear Friend,

In the City of Boston, the capital of Massachusetts, exists the Isabella Stewart Gardner Museum, home to one of the most notorious art thefts ever. Over thirty years ago, two individuals impersonated police officers and stole thirteen priceless pieces of art. They were all one-of-a-kind pieces, revered for their beauty and composition, and can never be replaced or duplicated. If you were to take a tour of the museum today, you would find empty frames in the space where the masterpieces once hung. These frames are a ghostly reminder of what once was. After years of investigation, the museum still holds out hope that these wonderful pieces of art will be returned to their rightful place—in the museum for all visitors to enjoy.

Priceless pieces not only hang on the walls of art museums; they also hang in the souls of people - the beauty of eyes that sparkle, a smile that lights up a room, or wrinkles on the face that express the wisdom of life.

There is also the inner beauty of a person's confidence, compassion, and humility. Just as the priceless pieces of art that once hung in the museum were stolen, so too can the attributes of a person's life - their value and beauty - be taken. They are left with a void, an empty space where their value and beauty once hung.

When items that one has worked so hard to protect are stolen, feelings of anger, confusion, and blame often follow. We relive the event over and over, asking ourselves, "What could I have done better?" or "How could I have been so careless or foolish?" The reason the art was stolen that night in Boston was because of their value and importance. And what made that art so valuable and important was the one who created it—the master who put brush to canvas, the sculptor who cast and crafted a masterpiece that would inspire, compel, or enlighten, bringing the viewer to tears, laughter, or reflection.

We have all been created by God, who on a canvas full of love through the brush strokes of His Word, formed you and me—God's masterpiece. That we are God's masterpiece gives us all value and importance. Genesis 1:31 tells us,

And God saw all that he had made, and it was very good.

We were created to be a masterpiece, but that also makes us a prime target for a thief. There is one who hates everything God has created. The first half of John 10:10 reveals the thief's purpose:

The thief comes only to steal and kill and destroy.

Thieves may not get everything they want on their first attempt, which is why we have all heard stories them returning to steal from the same place over and over. In the same way, our enemy, Satan, keeps coming back to steal the most valuable and important things from our lives until we are left empty, broken, and full of shame.

As a child of abuse, I (Mark) was groomed by my abuser to never say no. I was manipulated and brainwashed. 'No' was never an option. I was taught to believe it was wrong to say no, made to feel shame and guilt if I even attempted it. I believed that people would abandon me or be angry with me, that it would be all my fault if I said no. After my 'no' was stolen, I was left feeling broken and powerless. Even into my early adulthood, years after the physical abuse ended, it was hard for me to say no. Every time I did, I felt anxiety and guilt. I still believed people would be angry with me. Saying no still felt like I had done something wrong.

As a result, I said yes many times when I should have said no—especially when people came to me with excitement and shared decisions or expectations for my life. Sometimes I wanted to scream no! But I was too afraid; it was just too hard to say no. The awkwardness and disappointment others expressed when I did try to say no were a weight on me. That brought back all the emotions and feelings of being helpless. The no that I did express always came from a hurt place—a place of anger, frustration, or spite. I had to learn that a no could be healthy. No is honest, and it places limitations, respects boundaries, and enables self-care.

I remember my first big no. My past was trying to own me, the brokenness was trying to control me, and the lies were whispering to me, trying to keep me bound. My heart cried out,

> *Hear, O LORD, when I cry with my voice! Have mercy also upon me, and answer me. When You said, "Seek My face," My heart said to You, "Your face, Lord, I will seek."*
>
> **PSALM 27:7–8 NKJV**

Finally, with all that was in me I said, "No!" That no unleashed the helplessness, and restored freedom, power, strength, and confidence. A healthy 'no' gave my 'yes' a deeper and more committed meaning and made my yes even sweeter. I do not live with the inability to say no. Now I can say no because I have learned a 'no' is just as good as a 'yes'. When I found my voice and my no was no and my yes was yes, my yes shone like a diamond that sparkled. The yes became even more valuable. Simply being able to say no allowed my yes to be expressed with confidence and grace. I live my life in the promises of God, that are yes and amen

> *For no matter how many promises God has made, they are "Yes" in Christ. And so through him the "Amen" is spoken by us to the glory of God.*
>
> **2 CORINTHIANS 1:20**

Your words reflect your feelings, expressions, acceptance, likes and dislikes, what you stand for, and what you reject. I pray that your voice will always reflect who you are and what you stand for; that no pain or abuse will ever steal the voice God gave you.

A voice of one calling:

> *"In the wilderness prepare the way for the Lord."*
>
> **ISAIAH 40:3**

THE BIG QUESTION

WHAT WAS STOLEN FROM YOU THAT GOD WANTS TO RESTORE IN YOUR LIFE?

THOUGHTS, PRAYERS, REFLECTIONS

THE ROPE BRIDGE

Dear Friend,

When I (Mark) was eleven or twelve I became a Boy Scout. While my childhood was full of abuse at home and bullying at school, Boy Scouts became a place to escape from the daily hurt, if only for short periods of time. I always looked forward to camp! Even though there was never money to send me, Scouts always made a way for me to go.

Camp was full of swimming, boating, hiking, and an obstacle course. One of the challenges on that course was a rope bridge. It was the kind of bridge that was built with three ropes, two of them about waist high and the last one under your feet. I was petrified to cross it. Although the bridge was probably only about six feet off the ground, strung between two school buses, in my mind it hung over the Grand Canyon.

I was the last person in our patrol to get on the rope bridge. Instantly, I froze, unable to move. All I could hear were the shouts of the other kids mocking and insulting me, "Get off! You're slowing us down! You can't do it! You're too fat! Why do we need to wait for him?"

The words hurt and were all too familiar. They brought me right back to the abuse and bullying I knew all too well. I wanted to get down. I wanted to run. I wanted it all to stop. Then, through the cry of insults, one voice rose up. Louder than all the rest, my scoutmaster called my name. "Mark! Ignore them! Just listen to my voice! You can do this!" I stepped out onto the rope, not because I thought I could, but because my scoutmaster told me I could. Each shake of the rope under my feet filled me with such fear that I wanted to stop, get off, and return to the ground.

Then, above all the other voices and through my fear, I would hear, "One step at a time! You can do this!" Before I knew it, the end was closer than the beginning. I was only a few steps away. There was my scoutmaster with his outstretched arms, waiting for me. I did it! I had crossed the rope bridge! He gave me a hug and a high-five. "I knew you could do it." I did not win a ribbon or patch that day, but I received something of far greater value. By listening to his voice over all the others, I learned to listen to hope and love.

> *My sheep hear my voice, and I know them, and they follow me.*
>
> **JOHN 10:27**

Even though the abuse and bullying did not stop, I never forgot the loud voice that called me out of my fear.

During the summers when I was fifteen and sixteen, I lived in fear, paralyzed by a lack of confidence and a broken spirit. I felt like I was back on the rope bridge. Then I heard a voice, louder than everything else saying, "Come to me!" This time, I didn't hear the voice with my ears, but my heart. I knew the voice instantly. It was the voice of peace, hope, and confidence. It was the Lord.

On a rainy night, sitting in the passenger seat of my friend's car, my friend gathered the courage and faith to ask me if I wanted to receive Jesus as my Lord and Savior. Looking back now, I smile as I remember the two teenagers discussing God's love. We weren't eloquent, but God's love and mercy filled that car as I said the sinner's prayer, asking the Lord Jesus to forgive my sins and become my Lord and Savior. Jesus calls to us,

> *Behold, I stand at the door and knock. If anyone hears my voice and opens the door, I will come in to him and eat with him, and he with me.*
>
> **REVELATION 3:20 (ESV)**

God's voice, above all others, still calls out today, calling everyone to the love of God the Father and the hope of the cross through Jesus.

THE BIG QUESTION
―――――――――――――――

WHAT DO YOU HEAR GOD CALLING YOU TO DO?

THOUGHTS, PRAYERS, REFLECTIONS

FORGIVE YOURSELF OR LOVE YOURSELF

Dear Friend,

The phrase "forgive yourself" spark much debate in biblical circles. It is true that the Bible makes no mention of self-forgiveness. Simply put, Scripture speaks of only two types of forgiveness: God forgiving us and us forgiving others. Love, faith in Christ, and forgiveness form the firm foundation on which our walk with God is built.

When Jesus was asked, "What is the greatest commandment?" He responded with,

> Love the Lord your God with all your heart and with all your soul and with all your mind and with all your strength. The second is this: "Love your neighbor as yourself. There is no commandment greater than these."
>
> **MARK 12:30–31**

For a long time, I (Mark) did not love myself. There are many people who feel the same way after love for oneself has been stolen, lost, or broken.

How can we truly love our neighbor if we cannot love ourselves? How can we offer love, compassion, and kindness to others if we don't extend it to ourselves? When we are surrounded by darkness and disappointment, love can feel like just another four-letter word. Yet, Romans 5:8 reveals,

> But God demonstrates his own love for us in this: While we were still sinners, Christ died for us.

Christ died because He loves us. Like tiny rays of light breaking through the darkness of night, the love of God can pierce through despair and pain. Just as the morning sun grows brighter and warmer, replacing the darkest night, I believe God does the same in our lives. The love of God penetrates our hearts and becomes greater than all our hurts, disappointments, and fears. Accepting Jesus as Lord and Savior, learning to trust in God and receiving His gifts of grace and mercy is how I learned to love myself with an unselfish, honest, genuine love. God declares,

> I will give you a new heart and put a new spirit in you; I will remove from you your heart of stone and give you a heart of flesh.
>
> **EZEKIEL 36:26**

This is the kind of love Christ has for me, the kind of love I want to have for myself, and the kind of love I want to love my neighbors with.

While it's true that I was never told by family or friends to forgive myself—only God can forgive me—I was taught by preachers and teachers to love myself by loving God with all my heart, soul, and strength. God's Word and His principles are always true. Though giving love and forgiveness can feel difficult when there are scars, God's love is an unending treasure that fills and heals the empty, hurting places in your life. Allow His love to pour through you to others, smoothing the sharp points of pain, just as the ocean smooths rough rocks over time.

THE BIG QUESTION

WHAT DOES LOVING GOD, OTHERS, AND YOURSELF LOOK LIKE TO YOU?

THOUGHTS, PRAYERS, REFLECTIONS

JESUS PAID IT ALL

Dear Friend,

I grew up in a home where we really did not talk about finances. There was always food on the table and a roof over our heads, yet I knew my mom lived week to week. She would say all the classics, such as, "Money doesn't grow on trees," and "If I had the money, I would give it in a second." She gave what she had, but there were times when I could not attend an event because we simply did not have the money.

I wanted to break this financial cycle in my own life. There have been seasons of plenty and seasons of lack when I found myself saying the same things my mom used to say. There have been times when I needed help just to make it through the month.

During those times, while I was so thankful for the help and support, I felt trapped by the need. I would say, "I wish I could go . . . do . . . or give . . ." How could I change the situation? I needed help! It weighed on me. Rising above the feelings of embarrassment and shame, my inability taunted me so loud it was all I could hear. I wanted to fix it on my own, but God used these times to remind me of His mercy and grace regarding a debt I could never repay. No matter how hard I tried, I could never earn enough to pay this bill. Nothing I could ever do would balance the scales.

> *For the wages of sin is death, but the free gift of God is eternal life in Christ Jesus our Lord.*
>
> **ROMANS 6:23 ESV**

Everyone has sinned against God. We have all fallen short and made mistakes. The cost of our sin is death. He knew the price of our salvation before we were even created, yet He still chose us.

> *For God so loved the world, that he gave his only Son, that whoever believes in him should not perish but have eternal life.*
>
> **JOHN 3:16 ESV**

God sent His one and only Son, Jesus Christ, to pay my debt. The cost of my sin was payable only by death and the shedding of blood. Jesus Christ is the only one who has ever walked the earth yet never sinned. Jesus Christ, the Lamb of God who died the death I deserved and paid the price I could not pay. His innocent death paid the ransom for my sin. His death was the extravagant measure God took to redeem my life.

The financial debts I have experienced remind me of my greater debt. I needed help, even though I was ashamed and embarrassed. When I asked for help, it came. The lifeline was there, and all I had to do was accept it.

> *So we can confidently say, "The Lord is my helper; I will not fear; what can man do to me?"*
>
> **HEBREWS 13:6 ESV**

I am saved today not because of what I did but because Jesus paid the way to set me free. We are all works in progress, living imperfect lives, but we have a perfect God who sent His Son to save us all.

> *You were dead because of your sins and because your sinful nature was not yet cut away. Then God made you alive with Christ, for he forgave all our sins. He canceled the record of the charges against us and took it away by nailing it to the cross.*

COLOSSIANS 2:13–14 NLT

We are precious to God. You are precious to God. Pray and cry out to Him, asking for help, and know that the help will come to pay the debt of sin.

Let me leave you with some lines from one of the great hymns of the church, written by Elvina M. Hall: "Jesus Paid It All."

Jesus paid it all,
All to Him I owe;
Sin had left a crimson stain,
He washed it white as snow. [1]

THE BIG QUESTION
───────────────

WHAT ARE YOU ASKING GOD TO RESCUE OR RELEASE YOU FROM?

THOUGHTS, PRAYERS, REFLECTIONS

THE LAST STRAW

Dear Friend,

From a very early age, emotional, physical, and sexual abuse was all I (Mark) knew. It was the atmosphere, culture, and reality I lived in. Yet, some of the most painful moments did not come from a punch or argument, but because I was rejected by people from whom I least expected it. My home was so dysfunctional, rejection and abuse were so common; I became numb to the shock and pain. I was not raised, I survived.

It is ironic that a person who has endured so much abuse and neglect can be completely crushed by a single, seemingly insignificant event—a careless word spoken, a minor event triggering a rush of emotions, feelings, and actions. The final card that caused the whole house to come crashing down. The straw that broke the camel's back.

Junior High felt like a rite of passage. I was growing up and looking forward to going to a new school. It meant more independence, my own locker, and switching classes. I was maturing, and looked forward to getting involved in school in every way I could—sports, drama, and student government. I was searching for a place to belong, feel safe, and escape the dysfunction, pain, and abuse.

Let me share a little bit about my education. I have dyslexia and needed to receive special education services. I had an Individualized Education Plan, but one of the casualties of my upbringing was that I had to be my own advocate. Special education then was not what it is today. In those days, all special education students were placed in remedial classes; it did not matter whether they had a learning disability or behavioral issues. While I didn't move between classes as much as I wanted, I still had some independence.

At the beginning of seventh grade, there was an announcement that we were going to elect class officers. It was a big deal. We would have a president, vice president, and treasurer. I was 100 percent all in, excited to be part of something bigger and healthier. When they posted the date of the meeting and where the classes would vote, I was thrilled and couldn't wait to cast my vote.

The day came when we were supposed to gather as a class and vote on the elections. I waited and waited for the announcement, but it never came to my classroom. We never went into the auditorium, never heard about the value of student government, and never got to hear what people had to say. Later, I went to our vice principal and asked when the meeting was and why we had not been called. I'll never forget what he said to me: "Mark, we didn't call you because we don't call 'romper room' students to do things like that."

His words crushed me and brought me right back to the abuse and dysfunction of home. I felt belittled, shunned, and rejected. What hurt so much, and why I still remember it decades later, even with all the other abuse in my life, is that I never expected such words from an educator.

Since then, I have always been deeply aware of being marginalized, silenced, and rejected. The vice principal never laid a hand on me and never physically abused me, but his words put me on guard and left me feeling suppressed, silenced, and held back. They also gave me a heightened awareness of and sensitivity to others who have been marginalized.

Out of all the abuse I endured, his words crushed me, sunk their fangs deep inside, and colored my perception of reality. They rang true in my heart and mind because they reinforced the rejection and lies my abuser heaped on me. Yet, I needed to carry them to the altar and forgive the person who uttered them. Years later, as I walked through the valley of forgiveness, trusted the Word of the Lord, and stood on God's promises, I asked the Lord to help me forgive those who had trespassed against me—my abuser, my mother, and others. The statement from seventh grade resurface and this one story would come up. I would say, "Lord, help me forgive that vice principal." It took just as much faith to forgive that rejection as it did any other.

> *The Lord is close to the brokenhearted and saves those who are crushed in spirit.*
>
> **PSALM 34:18**

God is good, and He has been faithful. The straw that broke the camel's back, God redeemed and used. This made me more aware of who I am, gave me a will to fight and endure, and pushed me to persevere. I learned to never allow myself to be pigeonholed and to never give up. I laid my anger and insecurities at the altar, and I held on to the truth that God never gave up on me.

> *For the sake of Christ, then, I am content with weaknesses, insults, hardships, persecutions, and calamities. For when I am weak, then I am strong.*
>
> **2 CORINTHIANS 12:10 ESV**

THE BIG QUESTION

WHAT "STRAW" IS GOD ASKING YOU TO GIVE HIM?

THOUGHTS, PRAYERS, REFLECTIONS

PERSPECTIVE

Dear Friend,

In the 1980s we identified ourselves by who we hung out with and the kind of music we listened to. We found ourselves in social classes termed geeks, jocks, metalheads, and everything else in between.

I (Mark) would come home from school, grab a snack—usually a bowl of my favorite cereal, Cap'n Crunch—and turn on our local PBS station.

I had a love-hate relationship with that cereal; I loved the way it tasted but hated the way it always hurt the roof of my mouth to eat it. While enjoying my snack, I would watch the painter, Bob Ross. Perhaps you remember his big hair, gentle, peaceful language and soothing cadence. His expressions were full of light and kindness: little mountains, happy little trees, and clouds. I would watch him, take a blank canvas and, within half an hour paint what was a masterpiece to my fifteen-year-old mind.

The one thing that I remember most, even more than happy little trees, was that at the end of almost every painting, Bob Ross would add a big tree or some other object to what he had painted, whether it was a cabin, lake, or pond. It always seemed like he placed that big tree right in the center of the painting. Whenever he started adding one, I asked myself, "Why?" It seemed to block the view. Years later, I learned what he was doing—he was changing the viewer's perspective. Adding that tree changed what the person admiring the artwork would see, simply by adding one thing. He took the subject and visually moved it back.

> *So we fix our eyes not on what is seen, but on what is unseen. For what is seen is temporary, but what is unseen is eternal.*
>
> **1 CORINTHIANS 4:18**

Sometimes in life, the battles we go through are so close and so overwhelming it is hard to see or hear anything else. Even when we close our eyes, that battle is still all we can see and hear, no matter how much we try to focus on other things. The people and the events seem so close, no matter how far away they are. Even if years or decades have passed, it still feels just inches away, so close you could touch it. When Bob Ross painted a tree in the center of his painting, it changed the perspective. In the same way, when we place the cross at the center of our life and trust in Christ, the perspectives of all the situations, battles, or nightmares change.

Placing the cross in front of the pain in our life does not change what we went through or make the events of the past easier or right. It simply changes our point of view. Only through the cross and the promise that comes through Calvary, with our faith and hope in Jesus, can our perspective change. When we take the anger, bitterness, fear, and sorrow that tried to own us and give it to God, it helps us walk our journey with a fresh perspective and renewed strength.

> *And the God of all grace, who called you to his eternal glory in Christ, after you have suffered a little while, will himself restore you and make you strong, firm and steadfast.*
>
> **1 PETER 5:10**

Let us change our perspective by placing the cross of Jesus in front of our past, our struggles, and our future—always.

THE BIG QUESTION

HOW DOES PUTTING THE CROSS IN FRONT OF YOUR LIFE CHANGE YOUR PERSPECTIVE?

THOUGHTS, PRAYERS, REFLECTIONS

> GOD NEVER MADE
> A PROMISE THAT
> WAS TOO GOOD TO
> BE TRUE.
>
> —— Dwight L. Moody

COME TO ME

Dear Friend,

> Come to me, all you who are weary and burdened, and I will give you rest. Take my yoke upon you and learn from me, for I am gentle and humble in heart, and you will find rest for your souls. For my yoke is easy and my burden is light.
>
> **MATTHEW 11:28–30**

What a welcoming statement! "Come to me" is inviting, accepting, and open to all. The promise we find in Scripture is that we can lay our burdens down.

One of the expressions I (Mark) heard most growing up was, "Don't make a mountain out of a molehill." Sometimes there are mountains in our lives that seem so big we feel there is no way we can get past them, but then we do. When we look back, that "mountain" turns out to be nothing more than a molehill—a hill so small you can barely see it through the grass. Others are so big, so huge, that only through faith are they moved; only by the leading of the Holy Spirit are the mountains knocked down, moved aside, and dealt with.

When you have lived through trauma or abuse, walking on eggshells and always waiting for the other shoe to drop becomes a burden. Constantly having your motives questioned, your abilities doubted, and your confidence shredded while dealing with day-to-day pressures and demands becomes overwhelming. We become weighed down by the day-to-day molehills that loom as towering mountains.

Jesus never said, "I'll take away your burdens." He said, "Take my yoke and learn from me." There's a powerful lesson that Christ is teaching here: "learn from me." According to the verse, when we come to Christ, there are three things He teaches us.

First, Christ is gentle. When you have been beaten down in life and you are merely surviving, gentleness is refreshing like a glass of cold lemonade on a hot day. When we come to Him, He teaches us with a gentle spirit and encourages us to be gentle with others.

Second, Christ is humble. In the middle of our stress, burdens, and weariness, we are reminded of His humility. When Christ calls out to those of us who are weary and burdened, He does so while walking in our shoes. Sitting at the feet of Jesus, laying down our burdens, and hearing His humble heart is like finding an oasis in the desert.

Third, Christ teaches us how to rest. Some of us are so weary and tired we feel like we could sleep for days. We want to rest but don't know how. The worries and the burdens we carry are always chasing us, just a few steps behind, striving to overtake us. They are unrelenting, driving our thoughts until rest becomes unattainable. The weariness, worries, pain, and lack of rest pile up until we're buried beneath the weight. In Christ, we can learn how to truly rest, allowing our perspective to transform the mountains into molehills. We find confidence in a peace that does not come from man, but from God.

> *And the peace of God, which transcends all understanding, will guard your hearts and your minds in Christ Jesus.*
>
> **PHILIPPIANS 4:7**

How does Christ teach us these things? We do not buy a textbook, sign up for a class, or go online to earn credits. When my children spend time with their friends, they begin to adopt their attributes, speech patterns, comments, and inside jokes. They reflect their friendship because that is what happens when you spend time with someone; you begin to reflect each other as you grow, learn, and listen. This is how Christ teaches us as well.

The more time we spend with Jesus, the more we reflect Him. With gentleness and humility, we learn by spending time with our Savior Jesus Christ. We come. We lay our burdens down, and we pick up His yoke by spending time in prayer and in the Word of God. We learn to walk in His ways and embrace his principles. We abide in Him. As we focus on Him we let go of our burdens, and He carries them, strengthening us.

> *Remain in me, as I also remain in you. No branch can bear fruit by itself; it must remain in the vine. Neither can you bear fruit unless you remain in me.*
>
> **JOHN 15:4**

THE BIG QUESTION

WHAT MOUNTAINS NEED TO BE MOVED IN YOUR LIFE?

THOUGHTS, PRAYERS, REFLECTIONS

CHAMELEON

Dear Friend,

It's often been said there are two responses to stress, trauma, and fear—fight or flight. These are unconscious decisions, reactions, reflexes. When the fight response kicks in, a person may use their body or their words to gain the upper hand and win the battle. When flight kicks in, the only desire is to escape or make it stop. Flight can happen physically, emotionally, cognitively, psychologically, or spiritually.

There is another reflex called the chameleon response, named after the chameleon's ability to change its color to blend into its environment. The human chameleon response involves laying low, trying to assess what the situation demands, and fulfilling it in order to bring an end to the stress, trauma, or fear.

I (Jennifer) did not have the same experiences my husband did growing up; yet like a chameleon, I have found at times, in order to avoid offending people or tackling a situation head on, I compromised. Other times in an attempt to remain anonymous, I have done my best to blend in, hiding in plain sight. While it is true that we all have an automatic fight, flight, or chameleon response, we can consciously and deliberately make the choice to run to God, call on the name of Jesus, and walk by faith.

> *But you, O LORD, are a shield about me, my glory, and the lifter of my head. I cried aloud to the LORD, and he answered me from his holy hill. Selah.*
>
> **PSALM 3:3-4 ESV**

Trauma leaves its scars, but those scars do not have to be our identity or the quicksand that sucks us in and holds us down. We are more than just people of reflex and reactions; we are people of faith and hope, trusting in God, and confessing that He is bigger and stronger than our trauma. We are more than just mammals driven by instincts. We are intelligent people of faith knowing that God can make all things new.

> *And he who was seated on the throne said, "Behold, I am making all things new." Also he said, "Write this down, for these words are trustworthy and true."*
>
> **REVELATION 21:5 ESV**

Our past thoughts on survival were wrapped in fight, flight, or responding like a chameleon. We are not defined by the past, and we are not just a reaction. We are what the Lord calls us.

> *Therefore, if anyone is in Christ, he is a new creation. The old has passed away; behold, the new has come.*
>
> **2 CORINTHIANS 5:17 ESV**

Today is a new day. Let's put our hope in God for strength for today.

Do you not know? Have you not heard? The LORD is the everlasting God, the Creator of the ends of the earth. He will not grow tired or weary, and his understanding no one can fathom. He gives strength to the weary and increases the power of the weak. Even youths grow tired and weary, and young men stumble and fall; but those who hope in the LORD will renew their strength. They will soar on wings like eagles; they will run and not grow weary, they will walk and not be faint.

ISAIAH 40:28–31

THE BIG QUESTION

WHAT IS YOUR GO TO RESPONSE— FIGHT, FLIGHT, OR CHAMELEON?

What can you do to turn your response over to the Lord and allow Him to work in and through you?

THOUGHTS, PRAYERS, REFLECTIONS

WHAT THE ENEMY MEANT FOR EVIL

Dear Friend,

I (Mark) grew up during the time between vinyl records and eight track tapes, well before CDs, MP3s, and downloads. My abuser had music playing all the time. The album that continuously echoed throughout the house was the 1970s *Jesus Christ Superstar* rock opera. Even today, I know almost every word to every song. While the album was not written as an evangelistic tool or a witness for Jesus Christ, even questioning the deity of Jesus, the main theme revolves around Jesus, asking if He believed what people said about Him. Like every opera, the main theme is repeated over and over throughout the show. That song filled my home of avocado green appliances, shag rugs, dysfunction, and abuse.

As many songs, sermons, and people confess, there is power in the name of Jesus. While the *Jesus Christ Superstar* album was written to mock the name of Jesus and my abuser chose to play it in his defiance of Christ, that same song reminded me that there was a God who loved me, that there was hope beyond the dysfunction and abuse. There is power in the name of Jesus.

While I was too young to understand the mockery and defiance, and although the song played with the name of Christ ringing loud from the four-foot-high speakers, the abuse didn't end. Yet, hearing the name of Jesus Christ gave me hope and a firm foundation in the midst of the nightmare I was living

> But God's firm foundation stands, bearing this seal: "The Lord knows those who are his," and, "Let everyone who names the name of the Lord depart from iniquity."
>
> **2 TIMOTHY 2:19 ESV**

> We wait in hope for the LORD; he is our help and our shield.
>
> **PSALM 33:20**

Growing up in an abusive, dysfunctional home was like being on a ship without an anchor or a mooring, tossed and turned with nothing solid, firm, or secure. Without a rudder there was total chaos in relationships, values, and love; everything was manipulated and controlled. The ultimate act of rebellion from my abuser was playing this album—his soundtrack—expressing his anger at the Savior. The only thing constant was the abuse. The only thing assured was the abuse. On repeat like the chorus line in a song—the abuse. Both the song and the man that challenged the deity of Christ, used to justify this abuser's own selfishness, became a witness to me and a light in the midst of darkness. May a song ring in your heart that is louder than the hurt and greater than your pain.

The shepherd-turned-king, David, found comfort in playing the harp in the midst of war, trials, doubts, fears, and regrets. David poured out his heart allowing his praise to get louder, and through his songs, God gave us the book of Psalms. May you allow your praise to become louder, and may your psalm rise up.

> You intended to harm me, but God intended it for good to accomplish what is now being done, the saving of many lives.
>
> **GENESIS 50:20**

THE BIG QUESTION

WHAT WAS THE SOUNDTRACK OF YOUR LIFE?

Listen for the soundtrack God is laying down for you, and write down God's playlist that reminds you of who He is.

THOUGHTS, PRAYERS, REFLECTIONS

> THE ONLY WAY TO KEEP A BROKEN VESSEL FULL IS TO KEEP IT ALWAYS UNDER THE TAP.
>
> — *Billy Sunday*

LOVE LIFTS US UP

Dear Friend,

"Love lifts us up" are four words found in the chorus of the theme song "Up Where We Belong" from the 1982 film *An Officer and a Gentleman*. This film was released during the early days of cable television, when I (Mark) was about twelve, and it seemed like HBO played it all the time.

While *An Officer and a Gentleman* featured many talented actors and actresses, with some winning Academy Awards, the two characters I remember best are Zack Mayo, played by Richard Gere, and Sergeant Emil Foley, played by Lou Gossett Jr. One looked cool and the other was tough. I know the film had a romantic spin, but that part did not interest my twelve-year-old-mind. However, there's one particular part of the film that, even today, so many years later, I still find myself thinking about.

The drill instructor, Sergeant Foley, demands that Mayo DOR (drop on request) while granting the rest of the class a forty-eight-hour furlough —except for Zack Mayo. Sergeant Foley keeps Mayo back with the intention of breaking him before the weekend is over. The movie shows the rest of the class going out and enjoying a night on the town while Sergeant Foley relentlessly pushes Mayo, making him march in place while being sprayed down with a hose, doing pushups in a mud puddle, repeatedly demanding he DOR. Foley insults him, and reminds him of his shortcomings, failures, dysfunction, past, and family.

The climax of the scene comes when we find Mayo doing leg lifts, his legs in agony while Sergeant Foley yells that he will never be an officer because he lacks the character or the commitment of an officer. Finally, standing over Mayo in anger and frustration, Sergeant Foley demands the DOR and screams, "Why don't you just quit?" Mayo responds in a way that has stayed with me. He cries out, "Because I have nowhere else to go!" In my life, there have been times when the enemy preyed on my insecurities trying to get me to quit, give up on God, and retract my faith in Jesus.

> *For there is no truth in him. When he lies, he speaks his native language, for he is a liar and the father of lies.*
>
> **JOHN 8:44**

While the rest of the class went out and had fun that weekend, Mayo was subjected to abuse and insults. He was exhausted both physically and emotionally. In life, we go through seasons where we feel the same—physically and emotionally drained, while the lies of the devil scream at us, "Give up! Why don't you just quit?" During these dark times, we need to remember that the Lord is always with us.

> *For I am convinced that neither death nor life, neither angels nor demons, neither the present nor the future, nor any powers, neither height nor depth, nor anything else in all creation, will be able to separate us from the love of God that is in Christ Jesus our Lord.*
>
> **ROMANS 8:38–39**

> *What do you think? If a man owns a hundred sheep, and one of them wanders away, will he not leave the ninety-nine on the hills and go to look for the one that wandered off?*
>
> **MATTHEW 18:12**

When we accept Jesus as our Savior, we always have a place to go because our homes are built on the rock, the firm foundation of Jesus Christ.

> *Jesus is "the stone you builders rejected, which has become the cornerstone." Salvation is found in no one else, for there is no other name under heaven given to mankind by which we must be saved.*
>
> **ACTS 4:11–12**

THE BIG QUESTION

DO YOU WANT TO GO WHERE THE CHOICES YOU HAVE MADE ARE LEADING YOU?

If the answer is "No" What choices do you need to make to change your direction?

… THOUGHTS, PRAYERS, REFLECTIONS

YOU ARE LOVED

Dear Friend,

There are moments in life when we need to know that we are not alone in our pain and fear, or simply just not alone. We need the truth of God to counteract the lies whispered in our ear or screamed in our mind.

When the depths of despair seem so deep, overwhelming you with fear and hopelessness as your constant companions . . .

When you feel utterly spent, exhausted, and so alone in your agony that the walls echo with the sounds of your cries . . .

When your screams are so intense they become silent as the tears stream down your face . . .

There is One who sees you and moves heaven and earth to reveal to you the powerful love of a Savior who gave everything and withholds nothing from you.

Let your Savior's arms embrace you, for God hears your silent screams, sees your deepest fears, and knows your deepest needs.

> *And may you have the power to understand, as all God's people should, how wide, how long, how high, and how deep his love is. May you experience the love of Christ, though it is too great to understand fully. Then you will be made complete with all the fullness of life and power that comes from God.*
>
> **EPHESIANS 3:18–19 NLT**

You are precious and created for a purpose. You have been redeemed and you are surrounded with a love so amazing. You are worthy—worthy of this love, peace, and purpose. You are loved immensely, immeasurably, more than you can ever comprehend. In the darkest moments of your deepest pain, even there, you are cherished.

> *He heals the brokenhearted and binds up their wounds. He determines the number of the stars and calls them each by name. Great is our Lord and mighty in power; his understanding has no limit.*
>
> **PSALM 147:3–5**

Trust the Lord who walks with you through your pain, carries you, gives you strength, and fills you when you are empty. There is life, joy, and peace even during these dark moments. God's love shines through, vanquishing the dark, giving hope to the hopeless, strength to the weak, and peace to the anguished.

Beloved, God forgives our worst, most wretched behavior when we repent. There is nothing that you or I have done, or that has been done to us that God cannot redeem. God takes the rejection, death, pain, and ashes and places them on the potter's wheel, transforming them into something that brings life, blessing, peace, and glory.

> *For God, who said, "Let light shine out of darkness," made his light shine in our hearts to give us the light of the knowledge of God's glory displayed in the face of Christ. But we have this treasure in jars of clay to show that this all-surpassing power is from God and not from us.*
>
> **2 CORINTHIANS 4:6–7**

Turn to your Savior. Your salvation and redemption have been paid. All that is required is that you accept what has been done for you. Give God your brokenness, pain, and heartache. He is waiting with arms—scarred from the cost of our redemption—open wide to comfort you, hold you, and give you new life. As you take the first step, you will find that your Savior and Lord has already bridged the gap, no matter how far, and is right there with you.

Pause. Take some time with the Lord; cry out to the One who loves you with an everlasting love. Give yourself time to wait before the Lord.

> *Wait for the LORD; be strong and take heart and wait for the LORD.*
>
> **PSALM 27:14**

THE BIG QUESTION

WHAT DO YOU NEED TO SHARE WITH GOD?

THOUGHTS, PRAYERS, REFLECTIONS

GARMENT OF PRAISE

Dear Friend,

Do you have a favorite outfit? Maybe a pair of jeans that fit just right, a tailored suit, or a gown by a famous designer? It doesn't matter what your favorite outfit is, just wearing it helps you feel confident, attractive, and successful. Sometimes, wearing certain clothes or shoes can change how we feel about ourselves.

I (Mark) will never forget my bright yellow Tommy Hilfiger pullover sweater. It was the height of fashion in the 1990s and I was convinced the sweater made me look cool! I thought it made me look thinner—even though it didn't. I liked it so much I asked everyone I knew back then how I looked. Even now, thirty years later, when I see people from that time in my life, they will ask me about that bright yellow sweater.

It is amazing how a piece of clothing can evoke so much emotion. The way it makes us feel is why we will stand in line for hours for a special handbag or hat. An outfit can truly change our emotions and outlook. Similarly, in times of trauma, we find ourselves doing the things that bring us peace and comfort.

In Isaiah 61:3, we see Zion emerging from a time of sorrow. A word is given to them to encourage them that God is with them, and they are not forgotten.

> *And provide for those who grieve in Zion—to bestow on them a crown of beauty instead of ashes, the oil of joy instead of mourning, and a garment of praise instead of a spirit of despair. They will be called oaks of righteousness, a planting of the LORD for the display of his splendor.*
>
> **ISAIAH 61:3**

Isaiah instructs the grieving, broken, and hurting that even though the sorrow of ashes and the pain of mourning surround you, choose to wear a crown of beauty, be anointed with the oil of joy, and put on the garment of praise. The Lord's instructions are not for us to ignore the pain, but to ensure it does not overcome us. We are to stand on the one thing that's eternal, regardless of our situation— the Lord our God. We can find beauty in the ashes, joy in the midst of sorrow, and praise in spite of the pain.

Just as a new outfit can make us feel confident and successful, we are to put on the garment of praise and wrap ourselves in worship that is filled with grace. We don't praise God because our lives are easy or without trials; we praise God because, through all the trials, we know the Lord is with us. We know that the Word of the Lord lasts forever and God loves us. Jesus died for us, so we offer up a sacrifice of praise to celebrate what is eternal. Even when Paul and Silas were in the darkest part of the jail, after being beaten, they chose to praise God.

> *The crowd joined in the attack against Paul and Silas, and the magistrates ordered them to be stripped and beaten with rods. After they had been severely flogged, they were thrown into prison, and the jailer was commanded to guard them carefully. When he received these orders, he put them in the inner cell and fastened their feet in the stocks. About midnight Paul and Silas were praying and singing hymns to God, and the other prisoners were listening to them.*
>
> **ACTS 16:22–25**

Then the prison doors opened. As we praise God, the doors that imprison us emotionally and spiritually begin to open.

> *Suddenly there was such a violent earthquake that the foundations of the prison were shaken. At once all the prison doors flew open, and everyone's chains came loose.*
>
> **ACTS 16:26**

Even though our physical circumstances may not change like Paul and Silas's did, our perspective changes when we choose to offer a sacrifice of praise. When we praise God for all the things He has done, our faith and hope are strengthened. Our spirit is refreshed.

THE BIG QUESTION
───────────────

WHAT IS ONE THING YOU CAN PRAISE GOD FOR?

THOUGHTS, PRAYERS, REFLECTIONS

FAITH IS NOT
A CONCLUSION
YOU REACH...
IT'S A JOURNEY
YOU LIVE.

A.W. Tozer

THE BIG *BUT*

Dear Friend,

Oftentimes, when God calls us to step out and walk by faith, He wants to use us, to stretch and refine us. As those callings become clear through prayer and the Word, we often respond with excuses for why we can't:
"Lord, I would say yes, but . . ."
"But, God, I'm not strong enough."
"But, God, I don't have enough money."
"But, God, I'm too old."

The excuses continue. We are all guilty of putting something before our faith at times. It is simply the "big but" that keeps us from stepping out.

Believe me, I (Mark) am not pointing fingers at anyone; I am speaking about myself. When God called me to go to Bible college, I said, "But I don't read well enough. I'm dyslexic." When God called me to be a pastor, I said, "But how can I lead? I'm not a leader; I'm a follower of God." When He called me to write a book, I said, "But I'm not smart enough." I had all my excuses lined up for why I couldn't do what God was calling me to do.

I wanted to do something in my heart, but when I looked at my own abilities, the task seemed far too big, too hard, and too wide, so the excuses came out. The Lord reminded me not to focus on my own abilities but to look to Him for strength, wisdom, and provision. Moses and Gideon had their excuse moments, their "but".

God called Moses to stand before Pharaoh and lead the Israelites out of Egypt. Even after an encounter with God at the burning bush—where Moses was called, given promises, signs, and even help—he still made his excuse, his "but".

> Moses said to the LORD, "Pardon your servant, Lord. I have never been eloquent, neither in the past nor since you have spoken to your servant. I am slow of speech and tongue." The LORD said to him, "Who gave human beings their mouths? Who makes them deaf or mute? Who gives them sight or makes them blind? Is it not I, the LORD? Now go; I will help you speak and will teach you what to say." But Moses said, "Pardon your servant, Lord. Please send someone else."
>
> **EXODUS 4:10–13**

Through it all, God met Moses where he was. He sent Aaron to go with him. The answer to Moses' excuses was already on his way to meet him. Our God is faithful, and the people of Israel were delivered. God meets us where we are.

The angel of the Lord met Gideon while he was threshing wheat in a wine press, hiding from the oppressive Midianites, and He greeted him with, *"The Lord is with you, mighty man of valor"* (Judges 6:12 ESV). Even though Gideon didn't feel like the Lord is with him, God still called him to save Israel from the Midianites. Gideon responds with his "but":

> And he said to him, "Please, Lord, how can I save Israel? Behold, my clan is the weakest in Manasseh, and I am the

> least in my father's house." And the LORD said to him, "But I will be with you, and you shall strike the Midianites as one man."
>
> **JUDGES 6:15–16 ESV**

Gideon's excuse is one that many of us have probably used ourselves. "I am the least. I am not enough." The truth is, it does not matter who or what we are. When God calls us to do something, the only thing that matters is who God is. God is enough.

> [Jesus] said to another man, "Follow me." But he replied, "Lord, first let me go and bury my father."
>
> **LUKE 9:59**

We see another excuse here for why someone would not do what God called him to do. This had less to do with caring for a dying father and more to do with waiting for an inheritance, using family as an excuse to avoid God's calling. While we know we are to take care of our family, we should not use them as an excuse.

God called David to slay a giant, and He called Peter to walk on water. When their faith became bigger than their excuses, they accomplished incredible things because they trusted in the Lord alone.

> *Trust in the LORD with all your heart and lean not on your own understanding.*
>
> **PROVERBS 3:5**

I want to encourage you today to trust in the Lord, because He can open all the doors for His glory and use you to lift up His name. We all have our excuses! Do not let the excuses, the "buts", get in the way. Remember what the Word tells us: fear not. I encourage you to look to the Lord for your victory and strength.

THE BIG QUESTION

WHAT IS YOUR EXCUSE, YOUR BUT THAT YOU NEED TO GIVE TO GOD?

THOUGHTS, PRAYERS, REFLECTIONS

SAFE PLACE

Dear Friend,

We are all looking for a place where we can let our guard down, relax, and be ourselves. For me, this place is the sanctuary. The Merriam-Webster Online Dictionary defines *sanctuary* as a consecrated place: such as the room in which general worship services are held; a place of refuge and protection.[2] Both of these definitions mean so much to me. In church, I found a safe place—a place that protected me and gave me refuge. I have spent my entire adult life in church serving as a pastor, and while the church is not perfect, God is.

The church's doors were always open to me. As a teenager, I became a fixture at my local church, and not just for youth group and Sunday services. I was at almost every event. If the church doors were open, I was there. I probably even crashed a few weddings and went to a few senior prayer meetings, and I may have even shown up for the Mothers of Preschoolers group.

As I grew and matured, I realized the sanctuary, the safe place, is not just found within the walls of the church. While I deeply value the importance of the church and appreciate it as a gift to the body of Christ, the safe place we seek can be physical, emotional, or spiritual. The physical sanctuary will always bring joy to my heart, but so will the emotional and spiritual safe place of knowing that Christ is with me wherever I go.

> *And surely I am with you always, to the very end of the age.*
>
> **MATTHEW 28:20**

Knowing that God is always with me when I bow my head and lift up the name of Jesus, I enter my safe place, my sanctuary. It fills me with the confidence, peace, and safety that only comes from the Lord.

> *The Most High does not live in houses made by human hands.*
>
> **ACTS 7:48**

When Jesus died on the cross and the veil was ripped in two, God chose to dwell within us because of the blood of Christ, and in that, I find peace and hope.

> *And I am convinced that nothing can ever separate us from God's love. Neither death nor life, neither angels nor demons, neither our fears for today nor our worries about tomorrow—not even the powers of hell can separate us from God's love. No power in the sky above or in the earth below—indeed, nothing in all creation will ever be able to separate us from the love of God that is revealed in Christ Jesus our Lord.*
>
> **ROMANS 8:38–39 NLT**

Everywhere we look, we see God, in His glory, and there is safety and peace, even in the midst of the storm.

> The heavens declare the glory of God; the skies proclaim the work of his hands.
>
> **PSALM 19:1**

In our safe place, as we reflect upon the brokenness, trials, and battles that have tried to identify us, God reminds us we are more than survivors. Through the trials we have faced, we have learned to stand firm, hold on, and push forward. As we surrender all we've been through to God, we can thrive and declare with the same confidence that Joseph did in Genesis 50:20:

> You intended to harm me, but God intended it for good to accomplish what is now being done, the saving of many lives.

THE BIG QUESTION

WHERE DO YOU FIND PEACE AND SAFETY?

Search for and write down the verses that bring peace to your heart.

THOUGHTS, PRAYERS, REFLECTIONS

RETURN TO SENDER, ADDRESS UNKNOWN

Dear Friend,

Return to Sender, Address Unknown. Some of us reading these words can hear the familiar voice of Elvis Presley singing them. This is also the message stamped on an envelope when the person you mailed it to is no longer there. A simple note, "Return to Sender", was sent back to the person. The meaning was clear; we don't know where this person is, but they're no longer at this address. The mail you sent cannot be delivered; they are no longer here.

Today, with the internet, social media, and online searches, it is much easier to find people than it ever has been before. It does not matter if they change their address, get a new phone number, or move out of town. In some ways we are more connected than we have ever been before.

I thank God that He knows my name, where I live, and how to connect with me. When God reaches out to someone, they are met exactly where they are. There is no need for a "Return to sender" stamp. The Scriptures are full of reminders that God is calling us. There is no place we can hide from the Lord.

God always knows where we are, and in the truth of that knowledge there is hope and peace.

> *Before I formed you in the womb, I knew you; before you were born, I set you apart; I appointed you as a prophet to the nations.*
>
> **JEREMIAH 1:5**

> *If I ascend into heaven, You are there; if I make my bed in hell, behold, You are there.*
>
> **PSALM 139:8 NKJV**

There are times we don't want to be found. We don't want that package or letter to show up—the late bill, subpoena, or bad news. Sometimes we may even try to change our address on purpose. It is the same in our spiritual walk. There are moments when we just want to hide. But even then, the Lord finds us and calls us.

> *The LORD God called to Adam, "Why are you hiding?" And Adam replied, "I heard you coming and didn't want you to see me naked. So I hid."*
>
> **GENESIS 3:9–10 TLB**

> *Nothing in all creation is hidden from God's sight. Everything is uncovered and laid bare before the eyes of him to whom we must give account.*
>
> **HEBREWS 4:13 NIV**

The truth is, we can't change our address or hide from God. He is sending us a message every day—a message of love, hope, forgiveness, and grace to restore us. When I was away from God, He was calling for me. God is calling for you too. It amazes me to remember that God did not wait for me to call out to Him. He prepared for me, gave His life for me, and drew me to Him.

> But God demonstrates his own love for us in this: While we were still sinners, Christ died for us.
>
> **ROMANS 5:8**

The Lord never told us to remain in our sins. Jesus died so our sins could be forgiven. Wherever you are today, the Lord loves you and wants to be with you. Have you received the love letter God is continually sending? Check your heart. The Lord knows your address and is calling you because He loves you.

THE BIG QUESTION

HAVE YOU EVER SENT OFF A PRAYER TO THE LORD WITH YOUR EXPECTED ANSWER INCLUDED?

Spend some time with the Lord and look for the ways God is answering you.

THOUGHTS, PRAYERS, REFLECTIONS

> WHOSOEVER WILL REIGN WITH CHRIST IN HEAVEN, MUST HAVE CHRIST REIGNING IN HIM ON EARTH.
>
> — John Wesley

KNOW THAT I AM GOD

Dear Friend,

Simply put, life is busy. Responsibilities, expectations, and commitments all demand our time. We wake up to a to-do list of all the things we need to do and places we need to go, all before our first cup of coffee.

We run all day long, going from here to there, trying to complete a never-ending list. Sometimes we don't even stop to breathe until our heads hit the pillow at night, hoping for a few hours of sleep before starting all over again in the morning. Too many of us live this way, driven by busyness. But our health, our family, and our spirit pay the price.

When we are moving at that kind of pace, we know we need to slow down and take a break, yet we push back and say, "I can't, I'm not able to," and continue piling on more. Even when we finally go on the vacation we have been waiting for, it takes three days to unwind, and before we know it, we are back to running again. Being a hard worker is a good thing, but sometimes we can get lost in the busyness. It feels like we need permission to just stop and rest—to take a moment, to breathe.

When I (Jennifer) was in college, a professor gave me a wonderful gift. It was a tiny box with a little bow on it, and inside was just one thing—a pause. Sometimes I need a visual reminder to pause and breathe. Life gets so busy that I feel like a hamster on a wheel, running constantly yet getting nowhere. Then I pause and look up from the dishes to the small tile I've placed above my kitchen sink, which reads, "Be still, and know that I am God."

> *He says, "Be still, and know that I am God."*
>
> **PSALM 46:10**

When we hear this verse, many of us focus on the "be still". Our minds race, wondering what it means to be still, to be alone, and to contemplate. Soon, the busyness of our lives takes over, filling our heads with all we 'should' be doing. We give up, simply saying, "I can't." Again, God whispers in our heart, "Be still, and know that I am God."

God wants us to be still and to trust. In the stillness, we find God, and He fills us with peace, hope, and mercy. God gives us permission today to find rest in Him.

> *Take my yoke upon you and learn from me, for I am gentle and humble in heart, and you will find rest for your souls. For my yoke is easy, and my burden is light.*
>
> **MATTHEW 11:29–30**

> *And he said, "My presence will go with you, and I will give you rest."*
>
> **EXODUS 33:14 ESV**

My hope for you today, as you tend to your responsibilities, is that you find a balance between peace and duty. Find a place where you can sit in the sun, take a deep breath, and abide in Christ as He abides in you. May the peace of the Lord be your strength and hope, fill you with confidence, giving you the security that all will be well. You will put your hand back on the plow soon but take a moment to be still and know that He is God.

> *May the God of hope fill you with all joy and peace as you trust in him, so that you may overflow with hope by the power of the Holy Spirit.*
>
> **ROMANS 15:13**

Use your devotional time to pause and breathe. Take a moment and wait on the Lord. Let Him strengthen you and uphold you.

THE BIG QUESTION

WHAT IS DRIVING YOU?

Are you ready to wait for the Lord as He says, "Be still, and know that I am God"? How can you prepare yourself?

THOUGHTS, PRAYERS, REFLECTIONS

THE GOOD SEED

Dear Friend,

Being a pastor has given me the opportunity to meet people from many different industries, jobs, and careers. I've met small business owners, local contractors, long-haul truckers, factory owners, international salespeople, and many others. But the ones I think about most often are the farmers.

There was a season in our ministry when I pastored a church in an agricultural community. I quickly learned quips like "The corn needs to be knee-high by the Fourth of July" and "We need to make hay when the sun shines." What really struck me was how the entire community was shaped by this one industry. When you live in a farming community, you realize that the heart of the community and the pace of its daily life revolves around the farm. There's a romantic side, as you drive past acres and acres of cornfields and white fences, with horses and cattle running near a big farmhouse. And then there's the less romantic side, as manure is spread across the fields in the spring.

There are certain responsibilities when you live in an agricultural community. For instance, in the community where I lived, farm equipment always had the right of way on the road. The tractor and the plow will put a smile on your face as you watch the hard work of farming being done, but there are also times when you're stuck behind a combine and you need to get somewhere.

One morning I walked into a coffee shop and spoke to someone wearing ripped jeans, rolled-up sleeves, and a stained shirt, only to find out he had just leveraged twenty years' worth of my salary on this year's crop. The weather—rain, wind, and heat—all determine what kind of year the farmer will have.

Of course, as a pastor, my mind raced to the parable of the good seed in Matthew 13:3–9.

> *Then he told them many things in parables, saying, "A farmer went out to sow his seed. As he was scattering the seed, some fell along the path, and the birds came and ate it up. Some fell on rocky places where the soil did not have much. It sprang up quickly because the soil was shallow. But when the sun came up, the plants were scorched, and they withered because they had no root. Other seeds fell among thorns, which grew up and choked the plants. Still other seed fell on good soil, where it produced a crop—a hundred, sixty, or thirty times what was sown."*

Jesus explained to His disciples that the seed is the Word of God, and the soil is the heart of man. Sometimes the seed falls on rocky or thorny ground, and other times on good ground. Jesus desribed the soil and what happens to the seed in each scenario, but today I want to focus on the good ground. Like any seed that gets planted, it needs to be nurtured, cared for, and protected.

I believe that as Christians we need to protect that seed of hope, faith, and love that God has given us. The seed has brought us to a place of salvation, allowing us to receive Christ as our Lord and Savior, knowing that His death on the cross has redeemed us and saved us. But how do we nurture, care for, and protect the seed?

These principles have remained the same since Christ preached this parable, illustrating that we must be people of prayer. Take time to get away and pray. We must also be people of the Word, as God still speaks through it. Take time to read and listen to the Word, which is the Bible. We must be people of faith. When God says He will do something or tells us not to do something, we need to trust Him. In this soil, the seed will grow best.

THE BIG QUESTION

WHAT KIND OF "SOIL" ARE YOU CULTIVATING IN YOUR HEART?

What are the "rocks" or "weeds" that God is showing you need to be removed?

THOUGHTS, PRAYERS, REFLECTIONS

NOT JUST A FAN

Dear Friend,

I am a sports fan, and I have spent lots of time and energy rooting for my teams. I wear their team T-shirts and hats, and I have scheduled appointments, outings, and gatherings around sporting events. I have come home early or left late just to finish a game. I'm inches away from being the guy in the middle of January who paints half his body with the team colors. And I'm not just a fan of one sport—I like basketball, baseball, football, and hockey. I am a committed sports fan, consuming sports news as much as I can.

My teams have made me weep and have given me great joy. Yet, never once have I met an owner, nor would they take my calls. We don't hang out. I have never met the coach or even the players. When the team is winning and when they're losing, I call them my team. It is a passion that for me is enjoyable and fun. No matter how much I invest in my teams, I'll probably never be in a team meeting or see a playbook. As a fan, there will always be a bit of distance between me and the team.

The Lord calls us to be more than just fans; He calls us to be disciples. A disciple is a follower, student, and apprentice. Disciples obey God, receive the Word, and do what it says. We have access to the Lord. We can have a relationship with Him; He knows our names and He moves on our heart.

> *Know that the Lord is God. It is he who made us, and we are his; we are his people, the sheep of his pasture.*
>
> **PSALM 100:3**

The Lord guides us, directs us, and gives us His playbook, the Bible.

> *All Scripture is God-breathed and is useful for teaching, rebuking, correcting and training in righteousness.*
>
> **2 TIMOTHY 3:16**

We have a relationship with the Lord because Jesus died for us and set us free.

> *But God demonstrates his own love for us in this: While we were still sinners, Christ died for us.*
>
> **ROMANS 5:8**

The Lord has called us to repent, be born again, abide in Him, and follow Him.

> *Remain in me, as I also remain in you. No branch can bear fruit by itself; it must remain in the vine. Neither can you bear fruit unless you remain in me.*
>
> **JOHN 15:4**

> *"Come, follow me," Jesus said, "and I will send you out to fish for people."*
>
> **MATTHEW 4:19**

I enjoy my sports, and I probably always will. I root for my team and talk about it with the guys as if I were in charge. In the end, though, I am just a fan.

The Lord offers us so much more. Being a disciple is more than just being a fan; it means learning to live for God, following His lead, and being obedient to the Word. May the Lord fill you as you reach out to Him, because when you accept Jesus, you become much more than a fan; you become a disciple.

THE BIG QUESTION

ARE YOU A FAN OF GOD OR ARE YOU A DISCIPLE? WHAT ARE SOME OF THE WAYS BEING A DISCIPLE WILL CHANGE YOUR LIFE?

THOUGHTS, PRAYERS, REFLECTIONS

HE IS NO FOOL
WHO GIVES WHAT
HE CANNOT KEEP
TO GAIN WHAT HE
CANNOT LOSE.

Jim Elliot

GOLD AND SILVER

Dear Friend,

> Then Peter said, "Silver or gold I do not have, but what I do have I give you. In the name of Jesus Christ of Nazareth, walk."
>
> ACTS 3:6

Many times in my life, I have made the same confession Peter made: "Gold and silver I do not have." I grew up in a home that borrowed from tomorrow to pay for today. Finances were always a struggle. When I became an adult, my financial plans and habits were stronger than those in the home I grew up in, yet there were still holes. I learned to trust the Lord as my Jehovah Jireh, God my Provider.

I admire those with business minds who know how to invest, create, and organize their finances to bring gain to their families and the kingdom.

Our family lives on a budget and prayer. God is faithful, and He always makes a way. Money has never been the greatest motivator in my life. What motivates me is the call of the Lord and the people I work with. Because that is what I value, I have missed out and left money on the table. I don't blame anyone; I know the decisions I have made and their results. We have always tried to be faithful with our offerings and financial sacrifices, and God has also been faithful to His Word, providing in ways I could never have imagined.

> *Don't worry about anything; instead, pray about everything. Tell God what you need, and thank him for all he has done. Then you will experience God's peace, which exceeds anything we can understand. His peace will guard your hearts and minds as you live in Christ Jesus.*
>
> **PHILIPPIANS 4:6–7 NLT**

Of course, I felt the pressure of finances, the embarrassment of not having enough, and the fear of what-if. In those moments, I found myself praying and trusting, not knowing how what we needed would come, but believing that God would provide. I have always sought the old rugged cross. I have sat with a church board and been asked, "Do you have investments, and if so, with what companies or stocks?" As they spoke the language of finances, I felt confused and ashamed that I did not know more. I prayed and asked God to help me understand finances better.

As I thought about investments, I realized they are not just in stocks and bonds; there are also investments in people, families, and God. The return we receive may not be monetary, but it is always rewarding.

> *Do not store up for yourselves treasures on earth, where moths and vermin destroy, and where thieves break in and steal. But store up for yourselves treasures in heaven, where moths and vermin do not destroy, and where thieves do not*

break in and steal. For where your treasure is, there your heart will be also.

MATTHEW 6:19–21

Work hard, be faithful, and trust in the Lord. I pray that the Lord blesses you and your finances, whether you are struggling or successful. Either way, our peace and our portion comes from the Lord.

THE BIG QUESTION

WHAT ARE YOU INVESTING IN?

THOUGHTS, PRAYERS, REFLECTIONS

DECONSTRUCTION

$\mathcal{D}$ear Friend,

The late comic George Carlin made people laugh and think—and he definitely made them blush—with his comedy. In 1990, he performed a bit that dealt with language, euphemisms, and titles. In the monologue, he illustrated how different generations use different terms to explain the same thing. He did this by contrasting the terms.

One of the terms he discussed was the disorder discovered in soldiers during combat when the nervous system had reached or gone past its limit. When it was first discovered after World War I, the term was raw and direct, simply called shell shock. Over the years it morphed and expanded from shell shock to battle fatigue, operational exhaustion, and finally, after Vietnam ended, post-traumatic stress disorder (PTSD). He argued that by giving it a clinical name, it erased humanity from it.

How we identify something changes our perspective of it; language is powerful. The Lord created with words. John 1:2 tells us the Word became flesh. Both Isaiah and Peter tell us the Word of the Lord lasts forever (Isaiah 40:8; 1 Peter 1:25). There is great power in words and the expressions we use.

> *All Scripture is God-breathed and is useful for teaching, rebuking, correcting and training in righteousness.*
>
> **2 TIMOTHY 3:16**

Over the years, I've noticed similar changes in the words and terms the body of Christ and the church regularly use to express their faith, hopes, and heart. Many words have been reinterpreted and reapplied. When we change the meaning of words, there are significant implications. By altering the meaning of terms that were once clear, direct, and true, we open the door to confusion, ambiguity, and misunderstanding.

Currently, there is a term widely used on the internet and social media by Christians or those who once professed to be Christians: deconstruction. Apologist and author Alisa Childers defines the theory of Christian deconstruction as "the process of systematically dissecting and often rejecting the beliefs you grew up with." [3]

While deconstruction is not a term I would use to describe my walk, I understand the premise. I have seen, experienced, and listened to stories of people who came out of toxic and abusive situations where church was more about control than it was discipleship. They came from churches where rules mattered more than heart, and man-made molds mattered more than the Potter's design for His clay. I am saddened by the fact that people need healing from trauma caused by a local church. Yet, I have also seen people heal from this and remain with Jesus, faithfully serving Him with their lives today.

Yet, I despise this term "deconstruction" because so many people use it as a wall to hide behind when they no longer want accountability. In their search for truth and desire to shed religion and rule-based, man-controlled faith, they end up discarding the gospel itself, embracing an ideology or heresy disguised as "seeing Jesus for who He is." It is a redefining of Jesus, but not based on understanding Him through Scripture.

To claim that Jesus affirms all, never corrects anyone, and doesn't confront sin is a perverted, twisted view of Him. Too many have used deconstruction to deprioritize the Bible as the authority of truth, along with the absolute, God-established need for the local church, while still saying, "I love Jesus." We must talk about deconstruction, but we must also get on the same page about its definition before we can have a meaningful conversation about it.

> *Come now, and let us reason together, saith the LORD: Though your sins be as scarlet, they shall be as white as snow; though they be red like crimson, they shall be as wool.*
>
> **ISAIAH 1:18 KJV**

Many have gone through a crisis of faith—times when they wrestled, when I wrestled, when you wrestled, trying to understand "why" something has happened. So many things happen that anger us, feel unfair, or are simply wrong. A friend of mine shared, "Don't focus on the why, focus on the who—Jesus. Don't let the why cripple you. Focus on the who, Jesus."

There's a hymn that reminds me to keep my eyes on Jesus, no matter what happens.

> *Turn your eyes upon Jesus,*
> *Look full in His wonderful face,*
> *And the things of earth will grow strangely dim,*
> *In the light of His glory and grace.*[4]

Deconstruction makes me think of someone tearing down a structure that is old, broken, or useless to prepare it for something better. While we can wrestle with the Word of God—since it is to challenge, edify, and even rebuke us—God's Word is not something for us to tear down and throw away.

> *Study to show thyself approved unto God, a workman that needeth not to be ashamed, rightly dividing the word of truth.*
>
> **2 TIMOTHY 2:15 KJV**

Every generation before us has come to a place where they wrestle with their faith, challenge what they believe, and ultimately accept what God has said. Each generation has looked back at the one before it and said, "That is not the way I will do it." They looked at some of the man-made traditions and legalism, then decided how they would confess and practice their faith. They learned to spit out the bones and eat up the meat. It was a wrestling that was real, honest, and true.

Now I also see people talking about how they've deconstructed their faith and have walked away from what they once believed and no longer claim Jesus Christ as their Lord and Savior. That is not called deconstruction, that is called backsliding, walking away, and rejecting.

The generations before us did not lose or throw away their faith; they grew in it. They did not give up on God; they grew closer to Him. Maybe, like George Carlin alluded to, by giving something a new name, we have removed the person from the equation and made it so broad and clinical that we have lost the true meaning of the word.

> *"But my righteous one will live by faith. And I take no pleasure in the one who shrinks back." But we do not belong to those who shrink back and are destroyed, but to those who have faith and are saved.*
>
> **HEBREWS 10:38–39**

While there are areas in our lives where we may need to deconstruct lies and abuse, I can confidently say that you never have to deconstruct the love of God. God loves you, God cares for you, and God died for you. May the Lord be glorified!

> *Daniel said, "Let the name of God be blessed forever and ever, for wisdom and power belong to Him."*
>
> **DANIEL 2:20 NASB**

THE BIG QUESTION

WHAT ARE YOU WRESTLING WITH GOD OVER?

THOUGHTS, PRAYERS, REFLECTIONS

SLEEPLESS

Dear Friend,

I worked hard all day and was eagerly anticipating a restful night's sleep. I got ready for bed, turned out the lights, laid down, and settled in. Just before I drifted off to sleep, my eyes popped open. All thoughts of that restful night's sleep flew out the window as my mind replayed the entire day. Every action, every thought, every person ran through my brain again. Did I get everything done? What did I say? Did I hurt anyone's feelings? Oh no, I forgot. I didn't get to finish... Did I pray for...?

> *Do not be anxious about anything, but in every situation, by prayer and petition, with thanksgiving, present your requests to God.*
>
> **PHILIPPIANS 4:6**

I (Jennifer) do not like to look at a clock at night. In fact, if we are at a hotel and there is a clock, I either cover it or flip it over. If I hear the telltale tick-tock of a clock, I moved it to another room. I do NOT want to know how much sleep I am missing!

I have tried getting up make a list or complete a forgotten task. The problem with that is, as soon as I think I have finished everything and can finally sleep my brain pops up a new notification, like what happens when you clear space on your phone and suddenly all of the updates that could not download before start downloading.

> *In peace I will lie down and sleep, for you alone, LORD, make me dwell in safety.*
>
> **PSALM 4:8**

I tried to explain it to my husband, who falls asleep as soon as his head hits the pillow. A long time ago, before movies were available for download, DVD, or even VHS, they were viewed reel-to-reel. When the movie finished, the end of the film would flap. That is my brain. The day is done, but I can't seem to figure how to shut the reel down. A constant barrage of thoughts overwhelms my mind when I just want to fall asleep.

There is a story in the Bible where Jesus slept at a time when others could not.

> *When Jesus saw the crowd around him, he gave orders to cross to the other side of the lake. Then he got into the boat and his disciples followed him. Suddenly a furious storm came up on the lake, so that the waves swept over the boat. But Jesus was sleeping. The disciples went and woke him, saying, "Lord, save us! We're going to drown!" He replied, "You of little faith, why are you so afraid?" Then he got up and rebuked the winds and the waves, and it was completely calm. The men were amazed and*

> asked, "What kind of man is this? Even the winds and the waves obey him!"

MATTHEW 8:18, 23–27

The day had been long, filled with teaching, healing, and setting people free. Jesus lay down in the boat and went to sleep, resting in complete peace despite the fierce storm raging around Him. Where I could not sleep, Jesus could because He was in constant communication with His Father through prayer. He was not worried. He slept because He was secure, knowing that whatever happened, He was completely in God's hands. God knew about the storm, and Jesus had peace in the midst of the storm.

I hear you. Jesus is God, so He was not worried about whether He said the right things or did everything that needed to be done each day. He knew He was safe. And yet, we need to remember that while He is God, Jesus was also a man. As a man He felt all the things that we feel. Jesus felt fear, insecurity, pressure, and exhaustion, and as a man he knew how to rest in the peace of God. Jesus knows how we feel and is perfectly capable of helping us trust Him in the midst of our storms.

> *And the peace of God, which transcends all understanding, will guard your hearts and your minds in Christ Jesus.*

PHILIPPIANS 4:7

When I cannot fall asleep at night, I pray and give God all the thoughts running through my head. Sometimes, I will get up and read the Bible. Most of the time, though, as I pray, I start to relax and eventually fall asleep while praying. At first, I felt guilty about this, but then I thought about the times when my kids were little and would fall asleep on me. I never got mad; I cherished those moments.

I loved feeling their arms wrapped around my neck, talking to them, or singing hymns until they drifted off. If I feel that way about my kids, how much more does God feel that way about us? I can think of no better way to fall asleep than resting in the arms of Jesus, trusting Him with every joy and every storm that comes into my life.

> *Finally, brothers and sisters, whatever is true, whatever is noble, whatever is right, whatever is pure, whatever is lovely, whatever is admirable—if anything is excellent or praiseworthy—think about such things.*
>
> **PHILIPPIANS 4:8**

When my kids wake me with bad dreams, we hug, pray, and I encourage them with this verse as we take our dreams and thoughts captive and focus on Jesus. There are so many things that can leave us sleepless—circumstances, thoughts, fears and dreams. When that happens, look to Jesus.

THE BIG QUESTION
___

WHAT KEEPS YOU UP AT NIGHT?

THOUGHTS, PRAYERS, REFLECTIONS

CONCLUSION

We hope this devotional made you laugh, think, and pray. In each letter, we wanted to encourage and support you, not only where you are but also as a witness to where God can lead us when we lay down our burdens and weariness. We pick up God's Word and live by His grace and the hope that is found in it.

A mentor once told me that an "ouch" is just as good as an "amen", meaning that God's Word should challenge us just as much as it blesses us. Through these letters, our prayer is that you will return to this devotional, share it with others, and use it to spark conversations for support and understanding. One of the hardest things a person can experience is feeling isolated and alone.

When we are in the middle of nightmares and troubles, and the hurts and mistakes of the past resurface, we often retreat into solitude in an attempt to escape. Loneliness amplifies the brokenness, and bitterness causes us to withdraw further into the shame and pain within ourselves. The weight of it all leaves us so exhausted that we sometimes accept the emptiness as reality and live as a shell of who we really are—of who God made us to be.

Turn to me and be gracious to me, for I am lonely and afflicted. Relieve the troubles of my heart and free me from my anguish.

PSALM 25:16–17

May this devotional lead you to the Scriptures that shatter the lies telling you that you are better off alone, that no one has ever gone through what you are facing and nobody cares. I like to think of this devotional as a wrecking ball crushing the lies of the enemy and of the past, with each whack shattering a little bit of the hurt and allowing the light and truth of God to pierce deeper into the heart, all the way to the heart of the matter.

Your word is a lamp to guide my feet and a light for my path.

PSALM 119:105 NLT

God's Word is a light in the darkness of the world, and we pray these letters will be a spark that shines, guiding you toward the truth and love of God. We wrote each letter with prayer, purpose, compassion, and understanding, reflecting a God who reaches into the miry clay to deliver, save, and set us free. Our prayer is that you will find hope, peace, and love through these letters, which point to the salvation of our Savior and Lord, Jesus Christ.

WHY JESUS?

If you are asking, "Why do I need Jesus? Why do I need a Savior?" this section is for you. We all need Jesus, God's Son, because Scripture declares all people are sinful. Sin means to miss the mark. Romans 3:23 tells us that all have sinned and fallen short of the glory (the perfect holiness) of God. In other words, our sin separates us from God, who is perfectly holy, righteous, and just. God knew we would make mistakes, but sin has a cost, and mistakes have consequences.

> *For the wages of sin is death, but the free gift of God is eternal life through Christ Jesus our Lord.*
>
> **ROMANS 6:23**

Before we were ever created, God had a plan. He chose to redeem us through the death of His Son. Jesus conquered sin and death when He died on the cross and then rose again.

> *But God showed his great love for us by sending Christ to die for us while we were still sinners.*
>
> **ROMANS 5:8**

God has given us eternal life, a gift freely offered. All we must do is receive it. What does that mean? It means accepting Jesus Christ as our Savior by choosing to repent of our sins and put our faith in Him. If you would like to receive and trust Christ as your personal Savior, you can express your faith in Christ through this simple prayer:

Lord God, I come to you today and accept your Son Jesus as my Lord and Savior. I repent of my sins and surrender my heart and my will to you. Help me to live for you. In the name of Jesus I pray, amen.

> *And this is what God has testified: He has given us eternal life, and this life is in his Son. Whoever has the Son has life; whoever does not have God's Son does not have life.*
>
> **1 JOHN 5:11–12 NLT**

If you have prayed this prayer, we want to welcome you to the body of Christ and encourage you to get a Bible and read it. Look to the Lord daily and talk to Him. Find a Bible-believing church that preaches the Word, proclaims Jesus, and walks in truth and love. Make time for the Lord, it is important not to try to go it alone.

> *Trust in the LORD with all your heart, And lean not on your own understanding; In all your ways acknowledge Him, And He shall direct your paths.*
>
> **PROVERBS 3:5-6**

NOTES

Day 4 | Jesus Paid It All

1. Elvina M. Hall, "Jesus Paid It All," 1868, public domain.

Day 14 | Safe Place

2. Merriam-Webster.com Dictionary, s.v. "sanctuary," accessed June 21, 2024, https://www.merriam-webster.com/dictionary/sanctuary.

Day 20 | Deconstruction

3. Alisa Childers, "Why We Should Not Redeem 'Deconstruction,'" The Gospel Coalition, February 18, 2022, https://www.thegospelcoalition.org/article/redeem-reconstruction/.

CONTACT US

OUR WEBSITE
forgivingthenightmare.com

www.ingramcontent.com/pod-product-compliance
Lightning Source LLC
Chambersburg PA
CBHW060531080526
44586CB00012B/702